Anthony Holt MBE was a pilot and seaman officer in the Royal Navy for over 30 years, after which he began a second career running two of London's larger 'Gentlemen's Clubs' for nearly eighteen years.

He is married and lives in Dorset where he now spends his time writing, sailing and working as a volunteer Coast Watcher.

Four of Clubs

Anthony Holt

ISBN: 978-1-291-83500-7

Disclosure

These four stories are set in London's Clubland. The first three, 'An Evening at the Club', 'A Ghost in Piccadilly' and 'The Colonel' are all based on events that actually took place but the names and titles of some of the characters involved have been changed and as presented they do not represent real people. The fourth story is a work of fiction. It seeks to represent some of the difficulties that can face the Chairman of a Committee when he is trying to steer his colleagues towards the best interests of a club. As this is a work of fiction, I have taken the liberty of imposing a twist at the end.

If I have given an opinion it is only my personal opinion drawn from the information available to me and from my impressions at the time. There is no intention to imply criticism of individuals or organisations nor to do anything other than to act as an honest reporter of events.

Acknowledgements

I am indebted to my wife, Irene, without whose constant practical help, support and guidance I could not even have attempted this work. Additionally, I am grateful for her patience, good sense and support for me when I was spending much more time than I should have been in attempting to resolve the seemingly never-ending problems that surround busy Gentlemen's Clubs in London.

Dedication

These short stories are dedicated to two people. The late Geoffrey Wilson was a true and supportive friend and mentor from my first day in a club until his tragically untimely death. Miss Laurence Fonteneau was my Secretary and then Personal Assistant for over fifteen years. She was also my gate guardian and a staunchly dedicated and reliable ally who often kept the 'enemy' at bay.

Contents

An Evening at the Club

The trill of the telephone beside my comfortable recliner chair jerked me awake. I picked up the handset and held it for a moment while I shook off the fuzz of what had been a deep sleep. With my other hand I reached across for the remote control to turn off the television which was still churning away with some 'talking head' burbling on. Click. The screen went blank.

"Hello?" I said, uncertainly.

"Hello, Boss. I'm sorry to disturb you so late but I thought you should know we've had a little problem this evening." I recognised the lilting Caribbean accent of Louise, our Senior Night Manager and tonight's Duty Officer.

"But it's all now resolved," she added hastily.

"Tell me," I said. I was wide awake now and anxious to discover what drama was about to unfold, being acutely aware that even if the building collapsed most of my managers who shared the Duty Officer responsibility would describe it as a 'little problem'. I supposed they were merely trying to prevent me from expiring with an early coronary.

Louise was talking again and I listened as the whole ridiculous story poured forth. "You couldn't make it up," I thought, as she finished and wished me goodnight.

It was Trafalgar Day – October 21st – and the traditional annual dinner to honour the 'Immortal Memory' of Admiral Lord Nelson, hero of the battle of Trafalgar, was taking place in the Club.

The dinner had already begun when one of the guests arrived late. He drove up to the basement garage in something

1

of a panic, waited impatiently while the shutters trundled noisily upward, brought his car just inside and hopped out, heading rapidly for the dinner and leaving the car to be parked by the duty porter.

As it happened, this guest was also called Nelson. Unlike his namesake he still enjoyed the use of both eyes and both arms; but he did have a disability. He had suffered a severe leg injury and as a consequence he had modified the controls of his car to enable him to operate both the accelerator pedal and the brake pedal with his left foot. The car was a big, powerful Peugeot automatic; so normally it would have had only two control pedals. There would have been no clutch pedal. However, the casual observer looking down from the driver's position would have seen three pedals. This was because the pedal modification had been achieved by connecting a bar from the accelerator, across the footwell to another pedal on the left, beside the brake.

As casual observers go, you couldn't find one much more casual than the duty garage porter that night. Raj believed in putting into life the absolute minimum of physical and mental effort. His job as a garage porter was undemanding and he could carry out most of the jobs given to him, it was said, without engaging any brain cells at all. This evening he had breezed up to the car, slid into the driver's seat and pushed experimentally at the three pedals, failing to notice that two of them moved when only one was pushed. His job was simply to move the car across the garage into a designated parking bay so he started the engine.

When he had the engine running, Raj puzzled for a moment at the automatic drive selector, thought it looked a bit odd for a gear lever, and with his feet firmly pressed on the brake and the clutch he ignored the now screaming engine and shoved the lever into 'Drive'. The problem with this, of course, was that his feet were actually pressed on the accelerator and the brake since there was no clutch. The car started behaving oddly. The engine was attempting to drive the car forward while the brake was trying to hold it static. Nobody knows exactly what happened next but in all probability Raj must have eased the pressure of his left foot on the brake, allowing the engine to win the battle and cause the heavy vehicle to surge forward. It raced across the garage with the engine revving hard and rammed a small, shiny red Rover Metro like a demented shunting engine. The Rover exploded like a baked bean can on a stove. It assumed a sort of round shape and all the windows including the sunroof shot out of the car. The little car, still being pushed by the big Peugeot, charged forward and changed shape once again as it was rammed into a solid concrete pillar, whose day job was presumably to stop the building from falling down. The only thing that could be heard above the din of shattered glass and crunching metal was the high-pitched panic-stricken scream coming from Raj.

Upstairs, the dinner was progressing nicely and the main course, the traditional 'Baron of Beef', was being carried into the dining room shoulder high by four waiters dressed as nineteenth century seamen, to the resounding cheers of the diners. In the room above that, another smaller but even grander dinner was just starting. Two dozen or so Household Cavalry officers, resplendent in their red uniform jackets liberally dripping with medals and awards, were just sitting down to a five course, three wine and champagne extravaganza.

Raj had indeed lapsed into illogical panic. His hand still rested on the automatic drive selector lever while the Peugeot continued to try to grind the Metro into the concrete pillar, steadily completing the final destruction of the little car. In an ill-thought attempt to disengage the two cars, Raj rammed the selector lever all the way through neutral into reverse. His foot must have stayed on the accelerator pedal because the car changed direction and screeched backwards across the garage, while the driver stared fixedly ahead through unseeing eyes, his white-knuckled hands locked grimly to the steering wheel. The Peugeot's progress back across the garage was soon interrupted. This time the big car collected a beautiful metallic silver Mercedes coupé, the property of the Club Chairman. The Peugeot's rear end smashed into the front of the Mercedes and the two cars charged through the garage locked together, jointly heading purposefully for the water plant serving the building. The first part of this to go was the water filtration system which was destroyed instantly as the Mercedes ground over it. Next, the control panel of the garage sprinkler system was side-swiped, which didn't ruin the installation but it did switch on all the sprinklers. Finally the Mercedes bounced off the heavy duty pipe supplying mains water to the building before the car, once the immaculate pride and joy of its owner, was fitted neatly between two more reinforced concrete pillars. Unfortunately the distance between these pillars was about four inches narrower than the width of the car, resulting in further radical re-shaping.

At this point the engine of the Peugeot stalled and a deeply traumatised Raj opened the car door and fell out to lie sobbing in a pool of oil and water while the sprinklers continued to rain steadily on the scene like a tropical rainstorm. The garage was filled with a devils' chorus of car and fire alarms rendering communication by voice entirely impossible.

It happened that George, the regular and highly competent daytime garage supervisor, was still upstairs in the staff canteen finishing his supper. He raced downstairs, arriving in the garage at the same time as Louise, the Duty Officer. While Louise stood in shocked amazement, George added another snippet of information, namely that the Mercedes had been delivered back to the Club that day, having had every scratch, dent and blemish carefully removed as a precursor to its advertisement for sale in the forthcoming *Sunday Times*.

Between them, they began to recover the situation. The alarms were silenced, not without difficulty, particularly as the Mercedes alarm kept starting up again and again until the battery was disconnected. Raj was by this time sitting cross-legged in an expanding pool of oil and water, in a blubbering, uncomprehending state of shock, surrounded by the wreckage. He was judged to be in need of medical attention and was eventually despatched in an ambulance. Water engineers were summoned and the Fire Brigade was told they were not needed. Manpower was assembled to shove the wrecked vehicles clear of those that had survived unscathed; and finally, Louise retired to her office up on the sixth floor to summon a replacement garage porter, to phone me and to write up the whole horrible saga in the log.

She also decided that she had better tell the owner of the formerly smart little red Metro, now a pulverised wreck, that they would need alternative transport. On checking, she saw that the car was owned by a judge – in fact this was a lady judge but Louise did not know that, nor did she know that this lady judge was married to another judge.

Louise found the double bedroom occupied by the judge. She was somewhat surprised when a woman opened the door, and under the mistaken assumption that all judges are masculine she blurted out, "I'm afraid your husband's car has been involved in a terrible accident."

The colour drained from the woman's face. "Is he badly hurt?" she gasped.

"Well, no, it happened here in the garage," replied Louise, perplexed by the response.

"What!"

"I'm afraid there was an accident in the Club garage and your husband's car, the red Metro, has been damaged," said Louise, carefully.

"That's not his car, it's mine!" said the woman.

"But it says 'Judge Black'," said Louise, now wanting to be somewhere else.

"I'm Judge Black!" said the woman.

Slowly, her error began to dawn on Louise and she extracted herself with as much dignity as she could muster.

She went back to her office, made herself a cup of coffee and faithfully began to record the expensive events of the evening. She had just decided to go down to Reception on the ground floor to see if Saiful, the replacement garage porter, had arrived, when her VHF radio buzzed and informed her that Saiful had indeed arrived. She acknowledged this, tidied the papers on her desk into a heap and set off along the corridor for the lift. The time was by now not far short of midnight; but the evening still had more tests to offer her.

Louise pressed the button to summon the lift and stood back, waiting. After about a minute, the familiar wheezing and clunking announced the imminent arrival of the lift car. It stopped with a slight thud, the double doors opened and Louise stepped back in shock. It seemed as if the entire space within the lift was occupied by a huge giant of a man clad in all the uniformed finery of a cavalry officer. He stood swaying from side to side, gazing out with unfocussed, unseeing eyes, clutching both sides of the doorframe for support. He opened his mouth to speak but nothing intelligible emerged.

Louise had had enough for one evening so she turned and marched resolutely back to her office where she began to busy herself with more paperwork, first informing Reception that she would come down later. By and by, she became distracted by a distant but regular noise. After ten minutes or so her curiosity led her out of her office and back along the corridor in the direction the noise appeared to be coming from.

It was coming from the lift. The large cavalryman had finally succumbed to the excesses of the evening and had fallen forward face down, his body half in and half out of the lift. He appeared to be sleeping soundly, snoring gently into the carpet. The noise Louise had heard was caused as the lift doors repeatedly attempted to close, sliding smoothly towards each other until they encountered the blissfully sleeping body blocking the entrance, whereupon they would then slide back in unison ready to have another go a few moments later. Louise had no intention of getting anywhere near the enormous drunk so she headed for the stairway, calling Reception on her radio as she went.

Louise arrived in Reception. Then, with Saiful the newly arrived garage porter and the Joseph, the hall porter, she set off to resolve the problem of the sleeping giant. They reached the sixth floor lift entrance and spent a few minutes cajoling the man into some form of wakefulness, eventually managing to get him on his feet before helping him off towards his bedroom on the seventh floor. As they passed along the corridors some level of sobriety began to return to their charge, who then spent most of the short journey apologising for the inconvenience he was causing and the state he was in.

By the time they reached the door to his bedroom he seemed to have recovered somewhat; and while his pockets were being searched for the door key, Louise and Joseph left Saiful to finish the escort task and set off on other errands. The door opened and Saiful, who was as short and slight as his charge was tall and heavy, entered the room, directing the big man gently towards the single bed.

Later, down in Reception, Louise was chatting to the Night Receptionist and recounting the disastrous events when Joseph arrived back. As he passed the reception desk on his way to the Porters' Lodge a strange sound erupted from the two-way radio strapped to his waist. They all stopped talking and listened. The noise came again, and again.

"Hep, hep," squawked the radio, weakly.

It was an indecipherable woolly sound. They listened more intently. The receptionist said, "I think it's saying 'Help'."

"Yes," said Louise, anxiety competing with despair in her voice, "it is. There it goes again: 'Help'."

"It's Saiful." Joseph was already at the lift door pressing the call button. Louise slipped in after him as he pressed the button for the sixth floor.

When they reached the sixth floor they hurried along to the bedroom where Saiful and the large cavalry officer had last been seen. The bedroom door was still swinging open and the bed appeared to be topped with a mountain of scarlet, blue and gold. They could also see, emerging from under the huge body, a slim brown hand clutching a two-way radio. The large cavalry officer had collapsed once more and was now snoring face down on the bed – except that he wasn't quite on the bed. Underneath him they could now just discern the slight form of Saiful who had managed to release one hand which was pressed on the 'send' button of his radio while he was trying to shout "Help!" into the suffocating folds of red and blue serge spread across his face.

Together, Louise and Joseph heaved at the recumbent form on the bed until it rolled onto the floor and stopped snoring. Saiful staggered to his feet and said, with some feeling, "I thought I was going to die."

****

The gods of fate had not yet finished with the Club. The Chairman, when he had recovered from surveying what had once been a beautiful car, was invited to hire a replacement car until the insurance was sorted out. He was told he could hire an equivalent vehicle; but being a man who would not wish to take advantage of the situation and add further costs, he decided to hire the cheapest car available.

The car he hired was small and certainly cheap. The lady in the hire car office explained that the car radio was removable, so that when the vehicle was parked he should take the radio out of the dashboard and lock it in the boot. When he drove home to Kensington, he remembered the instruction and followed it carefully. What he did not remember as he parked the car in the residents' parking zone was that this car was not registered to a resident. Predictably, next morning the car was adorned with an expensive parking ticket.

The Chairman set off to Kensington and Chelsea Parking Control, fretting about his mistake. He was still thinking about his fine when he parked the little car near the office. He strode off to the parking office and forgot about removing the radio. Forty minutes later, when he arrived back at the car with a temporary residents' parking permit, he found to his dismay that the driver's window had been smashed and the radio was gone.

He drove home with his mind now focussed on the double disaster and, at a busy traffic lights, he ran into the car in front.

He came back to the Club next day on a bicycle.

A Ghost in Piccadilly

Trevor was a dependable, unflappable, honest and generally likeable individual. At some time in the distant past he had been a corporal in the Royal Signals Regiment but for the last ten years he had been working as a porter for the historic Club in Piccadilly. The grand old mansion, once a minor royal palace and at one time the home of a Prime Minister, was now a gentlemen's club. Trevor lived in one of the staff bedrooms on the top floor of the club and kept himself to himself. As far as anyone could recall, he had never talked about any family but he was generally thought to have come from somewhere 'up north'. The club staff was a cosmopolitan group and those living close together in the small rooms at the very top of the building tended to form the relationships of an extended family. They weren't exactly in each other's pockets but most tended to socialise together and in due course to talk about where they had been, the work they had done and where they came from. This could not be said of Trevor. He was pleasantly companionable but he didn't talk much about his past.

'Steady' was a very apt description of Trevor's character. He was a quietly spoken man and appeared somewhat reticent. He didn't mix readily with most of the other live-in staff, many of whom he labelled privately as 'foreign' and therefore beneath or beyond his horizon. Short and stocky, he was always neatly groomed and soberly dressed, and he liked an occasional pint. However, he didn't drink a lot and never when on duty; but he could be seen regularly sitting in a quiet corner of the Kings Arms in Shepherd's Market, just around the corner from the Club, or sometimes, when he felt like a change, it might be the Market Tavern or The Grapes. He would nurse a pint for the evening, or if payday was distant, then it would be a half. Very occasionally he might have a second pint, but this would generally mean that someone else was paying.

Trevor had started work with the Club as a front hall porter but for the last year or so he had been working as a night porter. He enjoyed the work and found the task undemanding, particularly since it meant that he could proceed at his own pace and he didn't have to deal with many people. He still filled in sometimes as a day porter, manning the front hall, checking membership entitlement and carrying cases up and down from the bedrooms – the 'chambers' as they were still archaically known. But it was as a night porter that Trevor really excelled. He manned the desk until the front door was locked at midnight, then he would set off on his rounds of the building. To do this properly, including the labyrinthine basement, the extensive kitchens, offices, bars, gymnasium, squash courts, public rooms and the bedrooms, would take easily two hours, so he would expect to complete the first set of rounds at about two o'clock in the morning, at which time he would have a sandwich and a cup of tea before setting off on his second round which he would need to complete in time to open the door for the milkman and baker at five o'clock.

It was on one of these midnight rounds that Trevor saw the ghost. He was on the second floor passing through the large Regimental Room towards the highly ornate Egremont Room, one of a suite of three elegant drawing rooms at the front of the building overlooking Piccadilly and Green Park beyond.

Trevor was walking around by torchlight, though the street lights of Piccadilly also spilled some light into the front rooms, making Trevor's torch almost unnecessary. He approached from the adjacent corridor, passing through the small, elegant Cambridge Room and then through the wide open double doors into the larger Egremont Room.

Following his usual habit he paused just inside the doorway, allowing his eyes to adjust to the twilight of the room. As he followed the beam of his torch around the room he thought his peripheral vision caught a brief movement in the shadows away to his right. He turned towards this, shining his torch; but he saw nothing. Trevor grasped his torch a little more firmly because he thought he might be about to encounter an intruder, and moved the torch beam slowly around the room, enabling him to admire once more the elegant cream walls decorated with gilded plasterwork. The torch beam sparkled for a moment as it passed through the grand crystal chandeliers that also reflected themselves in the huge wall mirrors. He marvelled at the opulence arrayed before him as he stepped onto the deep pile pink-patterned carpet. He entered the room; then he stopped.

Trevor shivered but he didn't know why. Then he realised that he was not alone. A tall man was moving silently across the carpet, away from the door. "Excuse me!" called Trevor, but there was no reply, although the figure did seem to pause momentarily. Afterwards, Trevor was very clear as to what he had seen. The man – it was a man – was very tall, over six feet, and dressed in a brown military style ankle-length greatcoat. He had a shock of thick, shining silver hair drawn severely straight back across the top of his head and ending scruffily over his coat collar. The figure had stopped in the middle of the room, standing still and silent for perhaps, Trevor said, thirty seconds, then had moved on with his back towards Trevor – who had by then backed away – so that he was standing near the big window, partially silhouetted by the light from the Piccadilly street lamps. Trevor started to call out once more but for some reason he stopped and just looked. The figure again began to move away from him towards the far wall which was adorned with a large heavy mirror in a gilt frame. The figure reached the wall beside the mirror, turned slightly, paused, then turned away and simply vanished. Later, when Trevor was answering questions, he admitted that although the figure had been moving towards the mirror, Trevor could not recall seeing any reflection in the glass.

I learnt all of this when I arrived in the office next morning. First John, my Deputy, stuck his head around the door and said in his usual light-hearted way, "You'll never guess what's happened now?"

"What has happened now?" I responded evenly, expecting to hear some litany of disaster encompassing complaints or expensive damage or some such.

"Trevor's seen a ghost," said John, smiling broadly and obviously pleased to be the first to get in with a bit of unusual news.

"Explain, John," I said, still deadpan.

John stepped into the office and eased into a chair. He gave me a very broad version of what was supposed to have happened, told me that Trevor was now upstairs in his room having spent some time with Paul, the General Manager, and finished off by announcing that Trevor was not a very happy bunny.

"Has he been drinking?" I asked.

"Doesn't drink," said John, triumphantly.

I considered this. It was not strictly true but close enough, I thought on reflection. "Well, he does like the odd pint," I said.

"Yes, nothing more," replied John, to whom drinking only a pint or two counted as 'not drinking'. "Anyway," he continued, "Paul is on the case and he will pop in later with the whole lurid story." At that moment the phone began to ring in his office next door so he disappeared without another word.

Paul was mainly responsible for running the 'Front of House' operation but he also carried a general brief for much else that was going on in the Club. A charming and handsome individual, he was what used to be called a 'lady's man' which roughly translated to his penchant for trying his luck with the company of any women who might favour him. Despite his responsibilities throughout the building, he generally based himself in the miniature reception office, where he enjoyed the very close company of one or two of the team of lovely young French receptionists he had hired. It also meant that he was aware of everyone coming and going through the front door. Paul enjoyed a high profile among the members and throughout the staff. In a former career he had travelled the world as a sessions musician for a variety of pop groups and had remained well-connected within the music business. In fact there were few businesses where Paul could not be described as 'well-connected.'

He was a fixer and encouraged by many of the members to make all sorts of unusual arrangements for them; and it was said that when prompted by just a short telephone call, Paul could bring forth anything the caller desired, from a bottle of whisky to a railway ticket. Fortunately Paul was discreet so his clients kept coming back, time and again. I knew he was enjoying his extra-curricular activities but I had quickly reached the conclusion that most of what he did benefitted the Club and I should regard his business with a Nelsonic eye. Sometimes I found it necessary to have a short informal chat with Paul in order to guide him away from some more dubious scheme. This was invariably without acrimony and I always knew when Paul thought he had sailed too close to the wind because on the following morning he would meet me in the courtyard, smiling a welcome as I parked my car, before helping me on with my jacket and carrying my briefcase. A young man of great personal charm, he was very popular among the members, some of whom believed he walked on water, and he was respected or feared by most of the staff. One other important point in relation to what he was going to talk to me about was that his father before him had held the post he now occupied, from as far back as the nineteen forties. Accordingly and with the support of 'Dad', Paul could be quite an authority on the recent history of the Club, and 'Clubland' in general.

Paul arrived in my office about forty minutes later. He seemed quite excited about the news he had for me so I indicated a seat and sat back while he explained what had been going on. First of all he repeated more or less what I had already learnt from John; but what he had to say next really made me sit up.

"It's Perky Bradell," he said, beaming at me as though he had just won the lottery.

"Explain, please," I said.

"Perky Bradell!" he repeated.

"Who or what is Perky Bradell?" I asked, now beginning to sound exasperated.

"Not is," said Paul. "Was."

I knew he liked to string things out and he always savoured the advantage of any knowledge that he had which I didn't, so with an inward sigh, I realised I just had to play along. "Okay, Paul," I said, "just start at the beginning and tell me all about Perky Bradell."

"I phoned my dad," said Paul, as though this explained everything. I just stared across my desk at him and waited patiently for the next revelation. It was not long in coming.

Paul had indeed phoned his dad and related everything he had been told by the still shocked Trevor. His dad had reacted instantly.

"It's Major Bradell," Paul's dad had declared without hesitation. On further questioning he had explained that Major 'Perky' Bradell had been one of the Club 'characters'. A soldier from the Great War, Major Bradell had an interesting history. Some time prior to 1914 he had been commissioned into the Dublin Fusiliers and then had been wounded and captured on the Western Front. In 1918 he had been repatriated with other prisoners of war, re-joined his regiment and promptly found himself caught up in the 'Troubles' in Ireland. After Home Rule was established the regiment was brought home and re-constituted as the Northumberland Fusiliers. Perky had settled down to garrison duty in the north and had joined the Club in the late twenties so he could enjoy the bright lights of London. He retired from the Regular Army in the early thirties and, being a life-long bachelor, he moved into the Club and became a permanent resident. As the years moved on Perky became something of an amusing eccentric fixture in the Club. As he bumbled about the place assuming the guise of indulgent uncle to the longer-serving staff, he was rarely seen without his greatcoat, actually a 'Trench Coat', which was thought to have been his principal possession as a prisoner of war. Regardless of the temperature, location, or time of day, Perky Bradell and his coat were inseparable; and it was the description of this as well as the distinctive hairstyle and great height that had convinced Paul's father that the apparition seen by Trevor could only be Perky Bradell. We agreed that there could be absolutely no way in which Trevor might have known any of this.

When war broke out again in 1939, Perky was still resident in the Club but he immediately volunteered to re-engage. He was accepted for second line duty and was placed in charge of an anti-aircraft battery in nearby Kensington. Before he had been able to take up his duties he was caught in a bombing raid on the Club. Although part of the Club was demolished around him, he was saved from serious injury because when the bomb exploded he had been standing inside a substantial telephone box which then stood on the second floor of the Club; and it was here that he was found some twelve hours later. This phone box had been situated just outside the suite of banqueting rooms which included the Egremont Room.

Paul's father had suggested that it was this incident which might have formed the attachment between Perky and the Club, and he had pointed out that Perky's apparition had re-appeared very close to the position where the old soldier had waited so long for rescue after the bombing. Perky had seemed to recover quickly from his ordeal and began to spend a lot of time with his gun battery as the raids on London intensified. And it was there, at his gun battery, that the veteran major was finally killed.

The press got to hear of the appearance in the Club of the shade of Perky Bradell and he became famous. The London *Times* ran a two-page spread having researched Perky's history almost from the day he was born, and even the New York *Herald Tribune* ran a piece. I was interviewed on BBC London Radio, and French TV gave it quite an airing. The *Sun* put a column one inch square on their front page under the headline "Posh Club Has Ghost!"

Trevor was upstairs in the staff quarters sleeping as usual after his night watch; but as soon as he appeared from his room I sent for him and spoke to him to discover first-hand what had happened and the surrounding circumstances. Trevor was still somewhat shocked and didn't really want to talk about it. Several journalists later asked to speak to him but he refused point blank. One week on, he handed in his resignation with immediate effect, gathered up his few belongings and left, never to be seen again.

During my private talk with Trevor I discovered the one single aspect of the experience which had really spooked him. When Perky Bradell had been killed in 1942 he had taken the full force of the blast from a five hundred pound bomb and his head had been severed from his body. That night, in the Egremont Room, the apparition had not only paused as it moved away, it had turned to face Trevor. But it had no face, no head, just a perfect helmet of silver grey hair.

The Colonel

The first time I encountered the Colonel I was impressed. In fact it was hard not to be impressed; and I think most people around the Committee table felt much the same way. Certainly whenever he decided to speak, usually by loudly interrupting the previous speaker, everybody stopped and listened. The fact that most of what he had to say was either fantasy or utter rubbish seemed to pass the listeners by.

Nevertheless the Colonel exuded an air of authority which it was hard to ignore. He was tall, well over six feet, with a slim, athletic frame and a tanned, intelligent face. He had piercing blue eyes and a small trim military moustache. He walked with a crisp, purposeful step and could cover short distances remarkably quickly, usually between bars, which enabled him to maintain conversations with two sets of drinkers in two different venues at the same time. This technique also allowed him to be absent when the drinking rounds came to his turn. But above all, the Colonel had *Presence.* And few members would be prepared to challenge his opinions and assertions.

The Colonel was a Scotsman, but he was the kind of Scotsman who spoke with an authoritative English public school accent. From time to time, when he felt the occasion demanded, he would appear in some sort of Highland dress. This would often consist of regimental style trews but sometimes he would appear in a kilt, by day or in the evening; and on these occasions he could be guaranteed to find someone to listen to the tale of how the *skean dhu*, which he wore tucked into the top of his right sock, had been presented to his paternal grandmother by a grateful Queen Victoria. This tended to increase the respect in which he was held, despite the absence of any reason for Queen Victoria being grateful to his grandmother and despite the unlikely probability of Queen Victoria presenting a little knife to anyone, let alone a highland lady. The Colonel had established himself as a 'character' within the Club.

I was intrigued by the Colonel and decided to carry out a little research; so I asked the Membership Secretary to bring me his file. She appeared in my office surprisingly quickly and handed me a brown folder with the name 'Colonel WG Carley LVO OBE' written in bold blue capitals on the front cover. I opened the folder. There was nothing in it. I looked across the desk at the Membership Secretary who parried my unspoken question by saying, "Not all of the filing is up to date."

"How long has he been a member?" I asked, gently.

"I'm not sure," came the answer.

"Well, approximately how long?" I persisted.

"Quite a long time, I think."

"Yes, but how long? How many years?"

"I'm not sure."

`We seemed to have returned to the start of the conversation so I swallowed my exasperation, thanked the young lady and handed back the file. She disappeared as quickly as she had arrived.

I decided to try a different direction so I waited a few days and slipped my question into a conversation with the Chairman when he next appeared to ask me if everything was going well.

"I'm not sure," he said.

I was thinking of a different way to phrase my question whilst simultaneously wondering why it mattered anyway when he spoke again.

"He's been on the Committee for a couple of years," he said. "In fact, I've been thinking he might make a useful Chairman of Membership. What do you think?"

I had not been in post long enough to form an opinion on the matter so I tried to frame an answer which would suggest that I was not opposed to the idea in principle.

"Well…" I said, but I didn't get any further.

"Good!" said the Chairman cheerily. "Well, I'm glad that's settled. Come down to the bar and have a drink."

We strolled across the courtyard and down to the bar. The Chairman was soon surrounded by the usual gaggle of members, all acutely aware that tradition dictated that the Chairman was expected to buy the drinks when two or three are gathered together in his presence – in the bar, that is.

I made my excuses and set off to see if I could track down the new Chairman Elect of the Membership Committee. I failed. He hadn't been seen in the Club all week.

****

In fact it was another week and a half before my path crossed that of the Colonel. The General Committee assembled at eleven o'clock on the Wednesday morning and I waited patiently, shuffling my papers about while sixteen men, all bar two clad in sober grey city suits, greeted each other and pretended they were all friends and well-acquainted. The two 'non-suits' were the Colonel who was, as usual, clad in highland tweed; and another man, Matthew, wearing a blue blazer and grey trousers.

At length the Chairman took his place at the head of the long table, rapped a gavel on the polished mahogany and called the meeting to order. I had various reports to give which tended to occupy my concentration, until I was suddenly surprised to hear the Chairman raising the subject of the need to appoint one of the members to the important position of Chairman of the Membership Committee. Almost immediately the formality of the meeting descended into a series of individual conversations. Again, the gavel struck the polished mahogany and I winced on behalf of the Housekeeper.

The Chairman was speaking again and the members had lapsed into an attendant respectful hush. "What do you think, Charles?" He indicated the Vice-Chairman, a bulky, florid-faced individual with an incongruous shock of silver-grey hair.

It quickly became clear that the Vice-Chairman, a retired admiral well-skilled in the art of committee manipulation, had been primed. He didn't hesitate. "We need a senior member of the Committee…" he intoned, while I wondered who that might be, since they were all supposed to be broadly equal.

The retired admiral droned on, ignoring whispered retorts from various points. "I would suggest a military man. After all, I know, from when I was running it, that it's not all a bed of roses. You've got to know your stuff to get the right chaps in. Identify the bounders and make sure you keep the buggers out. Then there's discipline." He paused, fished in his pocket for a pipe, realised that smoking was banned in the meeting, put the pipe on the table and continued. "If a chap misbehaves, gets pissed or whatever, you've got to deal with him…"

A voice from my right said, just loud enough to be heard, "Keel haul them, I imagine…"

The Chairman glared down the length of the table, silencing the irreverence, which I realised had come from Matthew, an avuncular, easy-going man who had been one of the first to welcome me into my new appointment and who often popped into the office for a friendly chat, usually concluded with a large whisky.

The admiral was warming to his task, citing examples of bounders, cads and other forms of low-life: "…fact is that what a chap does, how he eats his food, how he drinks, his wife… all reflect on the club. You take responsibility. You take responsibility for what he does, how he behaves. We don't want any 'rankers', ye know…"

The Chairman had had enough. "Well, I believe you may have a name in mind, Charles?" he said. We all waited.

The Vice-Chairman picked up his pipe, fingered it, put it down and sat staring ahead, apparently confident that his task was finished. I saw the Chairman's lips move as he leaned towards the garrulous old buffer. "Ah, yes," said the admiral. "It should be Andrew!"

Everybody looked puzzled. Among those seated around the table there was nobody called Andrew. I saw the Chairman frown. He leaned towards the Vice-Chairman and I saw his lips move again. The admiral sat upright, startled. "William," he said, "I meant William." The buzz of conversation resumed briefly until it was cut short by the gavel.

The Chairman peered down the table, focussing on someone to my right. He beamed and said, "Well, we have a proposal. Unless anyone has any objection I am happy to endorse that." He beamed again, and I realised that he was directing his gaze towards the Colonel a few places to my right.

No one objected to the proposed appointment; and the Colonel closed the matter with a short speech accepting the honour and expressing his determination to carry out the onerous duties to the benefit of the Club and without fear or favour.

We all appeared pleased that we had a new and highly regarded Chairman of Membership. As the congratulations were voiced from each quarter a small, folded slip of paper was slid across the table towards me from a small portly man with a walrus moustache, seated opposite. I opened the paper. The scribbled note said, "Who the bloody hell is he?" I wrote my answer carefully underneath the remark: "The new Chairman of the Membership Committee," and slid it back across the table.

****

It was from this point on that the Colonel became overbearingly unbearable. Having appointed a couple of nonentities to assist him with his Membership Committee business, he began to hold frequent committee meetings, increasing his remit to include entertainment, bar opening hours, members' behaviour and appearance and a host of other things. He scrutinised application forms, often summoning unfortunate applicants before him and rejecting out of hand those he took a dislike to for any reason, often unstated.

One day the Colonel strolled into the bar while I was chatting to Matthew who, continuing his regular supportive visits to my office, had become a good friend.

"Ah," said the Colonel, "there you are." He spoke in a patronising manner that suggested I should have been somewhere else. Matthew slid a second whisky in front of me.

"You've met my wife, of course?" I hadn't, and said so.

"Well, you must. I've arranged for her to come to the Club, next Tuesday morning. Ten-thirty. You can show her round. Take an hour and a half and then we shall have lunch."

In struggling to keep the Club afloat, I was very busy at this time and the presumptuous imposition left me feeling frustrated and angry. I stood, wondering how I could get out of the lunch invitation, when I suddenly realised from what the Colonel was saying that lunch did not include me. I ignored the rudeness of the conversation and was on the point of leaving to join Matthew in a snack lunch when the Colonel leaned towards me, swamping me with whisky fumes, and in a stage whisper informed me that "You will of course address her as Lady Carley, won't you. She likes to use her title. Belgian you know."

By the following Tuesday morning I had curbed my frustration; and precisely at the appointed hour of ten-thirty I stationed myself in the front hall, ready to receive Lady Carley.

Shortly after eleven o'clock a slim, handsome, middle-aged woman breezed through the door, ignoring the greeting of the hall porter. I introduced myself and we began the tour of the Club. I had done many such tours for various reasons and I knew the full tour would take barely an hour. To make it last the required hour and a half I had to slow down and add interesting anecdotes and snippets of Club history; and even then I had completed the task, taken the 'guest' to the Ladies' Bar and bought her a drink, with nearly ten minutes to spare.

I was very pleased to complete the tour and hand her back to her husband because she behaved in a grand, imperious and disdainful manner more fitting to a pre-revolution French aristocrat than a twentieth century lady guest. In short, she was horrible; and I was glad to get shot of her.

A week later I had forgotten about the irritating tour of the Club with the Colonel's wife when my secretary brought a hand-written letter in to me. "You'd better see this," she said, looking worried.

I took the two sheets of headed blue notepaper and stared at them open-mouthed. I was shocked and outraged. The letter was a rude reprimand, criticising me for failing to send Mrs Carley (I had discovered by now that she had no title!) a letter of grateful thanks for her graciously having allowed me to show her round the Club.

Looking back on the incident later, I realised that here was the first sign of the Colonel becoming really unhinged.

I had a word with the Chairman and together we decided that the letter was best ignored. In fact it was about three weeks later that, encountering the Colonel by chance in the front hall, I wished him good day and enquired politely after his wife. The response was spontaneous and explosive. "That bitch!" he said. "She's gone and I never want to set eyes on her again." That was only the start of the tirade of invective directed towards the sometime Lady Carley. He was still listing her shortcomings as he disappeared inside the bar. I must say, from my brief acquaintance with her, I felt inclined to agree with him.

It was only a few weeks thereafter that we heard of the divorce – and only very shortly after the divorce that we heard of the new girlfriend. A lovely lady who, the Colonel said, had herself been dragged unreasonably and unfairly through the divorce courts. The Colonel was just gallantly helping her to get over the trauma.

I often had to work late in the evening. That is the nature of running any complex hospitality business. It was on one such evening that the Colonel next came to call. The Club was quiet, the restaurants were coming to the end of the evening's business and most of the members had either retired to their rooms or had gone home. My door creaked open a little and the familiar moustached face peered through the gap around the door.

"Good evening!" said the Colonel, cheerily.

I looked up and put down my pen. "Good evening, Colonel," I replied. "How can I help?"

"Oh, not so formal; never mind the 'Colonel'," he said, followed by – or so I thought – "Not a real rank anyhow; not the same as you, y' know."

I deduced from this that he was telling me that his commission was in the Territorial Army; however, I did not react to the remark.

The door opened further and he stepped through it into the office. "I was wondering if you have a telephone directory," he said.

"Certainly, they're in the outer office. I'll show you." I eased past him, leading him out to my secretary's office where a shelf held the entire collection of Greater London telephone directories. "What name are you looking for?"

"Not sure," he said.

"Oh."

"Yes, I'm trying to find the number of my flat," he said. The news that he owned a flat in London came as something of a surprise, and it didn't gel with the facts that he allegedly lived in Edinburgh and stayed in the Club when in London.

"Do you know the address? We might get that from Directory Enquiries." My hand hovered over one of the telephones.

"Not sure of the address," he said, looking and sounding slightly embarrassed for the first time.

"Um, that's a bit tricky," I said, while I pondered the situation surrounding a person who is unaware of his own telephone number, his address and the name of the occupant – which, taking his comments at face value, was presumably himself.

"Well, thanks, I'll just have to go there." With that he turned on his heel and disappeared.

I walked slowly back into my office, wondering how he was going to get to his flat if he didn't know the address. Maybe, I thought, he had a photographic memory for the location of the flat. I paused by my secretary's desk and glanced at the bedroom occupancy list sitting there. My eye fell immediately upon the name of the Colonel. He was shown as resident in one of our single bedrooms.

It took a couple of weeks for the penny to drop. The Colonel had by then engaged the services of a prominent and successful lawyer who was also a member of the Club. The Colonel had also taken the opportunity to be more closely on hand to offer advice on divorce proceedings to his new girlfriend, and had taken up occasional occupancy of the lady's flat. Despite what had been said previously, the divorce was still ongoing. His new lady, now being introduced as his fiancée, began to be seen regularly in the Club, frequently taking lunch with her new protector and his – their – lawyer.

I was having lunch with my friend Matthew at a nearby table when I became a reluctant witness to the conclusion of some financial arrangements. "I will, of course, guarantee to cover all costs," said the Colonel. "In fact, if I have to, I'll sell my Purdeys; but it won't come to that and I'm damn sure you will get paid." This was said in his usual unmistakeable parade ground voice. His luncheon companions looked down and concentrated on their Dover soles. Apparently the Colonel owned a matched pair of valuable Purdey shotguns.

Matthew looked up from his lunch and said, quietly and cryptically, "That's interesting. We'll see, won't we?" I wasn't sure what he was talking about; but it wasn't long before I was enlightened.

****

Over the next couple of months, three significant events served to ensure that the Colonel was never far from my mind. The first of these took place during a meeting of the General Committee. Some months previously an air accident had taken place over the Scottish Highlands. There had been several fatalities and plans for a memorial service at the crash site had been announced. For some reason, towards the end of the meeting the Committee had begun to discuss this.

The familiar voice cut in. "I invited them to hold it on my land, you know. Plenty of space, access good, but not possible apparently." Around the table images formed in various minds of the tall Laird in his kilt, striding through the heather followed by his faithful servants, stalker's thumb-stick in hand, deer rifle under the other arm, gimlet blue eyes searching the vast horizon for one of his hundreds of stags.

Across the table, one pair of eyes had rolled up, on a face full of disdain and disbelief. Matthew was not convinced. The meeting broke up and on the way out Matthew caught my arm and said, "I'll tell you about that later."

Ten days after this, a meeting of the Membership Committee took place. The Colonel was in the chair and, after the usual presentation of membership statistics, joiners and leavers and so forth, the principal item on the agenda was a disciplinary complaint against one young member. The young man concerned was unusual in that he had never held a commission in the armed forces so in one sense the fact that he had been able to become a member was a bit of a mystery.

The young man, a bachelor, was a civil servant who worked as some sort of clerk providing administrative support to members of the House of Lords. He was a strange individual, short, chubby and uninspiring but who spent a lot of time in the Club. His work in the House of Lords seemed to have generated inappropriate feelings of grandeur within the young man and this had further manifested itself in boorish behaviour in the Club, including the penning of rude notes, usually on the grandly headed notepaper of some noble lord or other. As well as being inappropriate and pointedly rude, the notes were normally handwritten in thick purple ink and addressed to the more senior members. Complaints had been made and were about to be investigated.

The Membership Committee assembled around a long table in the Cavalry Room. The Colonel, as Chairman, placed himself at the end of the table furthest from the room entrance. He was flanked on either side by four other members of his committee, one of whom had been co-opted for the occasion. I placed myself halfway down the long side of the table with my papers in front of me, and wondered whether the newcomer, a military man, had been brought in to administer punishment.

The Colonel had taken his place. He shuffled his papers and looked stern. He was immaculately dressed and exuded an aura which dominated the room. "Bring him in." He issued

28

this order to no one in particular. One of the committee members seated on the opposite side of the table to me stood up and strode to the door. The room remained silent.

The door opened and the young man entered, accompanied by the committee member who returned to his seat at the far end of the table. The young man was smiling and nodding towards the assemblage, and seemed to regard the process as a bit of a game. He looked around for a chair and reached out to draw one towards him.

"Stand where you are!" The Colonel had uncoiled like a pre-striking cobra from his seat and he now stood towering over his end of the table, leaning slightly forward, outstretched fingers just touching the polished wood. "You, sir, are a cad, a bounder" (he pronounced it 'bainder'). "You are not worthy of this club, sir. What have you got to say? Eh? Eh?"

An Adam's apple bobbed visibly and rapidly at the other end of the table. It was not a game. The young man started to speak: "But I... um, I..."

"Shuddup!" roared the Colonel. His whole body quivered as he continued, "In my regiment I'd have you broken, horse-whipped, d'ye hear? Yer sword 'ud be broken and yer badges torn off, ye bastard..." The last word was accompanied by a shower of spittle as the Colonel began to move menacingly away from his chair and slowly down the side of the table, opening and closing his fists as he went.

The young miscreant had begun to tremble. He looked at the Colonel, then began to move backward, glancing towards the door.

"Stand still! Ye bastard!" More spittle – and I would swear that the crystal chandelier shivered. The Colonel continued his steady progress down the table, the stream of invective undiminished. "Lock the bloody door!" he yelled. "Call yerself an officer? Yer a shit, sir, a piece of shit, I tell ye!"

The other members of the committee sat transfixed. I wondered if I should stage a rescue mission.

The invective continued until the Colonel arrived to stand a yard in front of his victim. The victim stood, trembling and sweating, eyes darting back and forth, searching for escape. The Colonel leaned forward. "Take that Club tie off; yer not worthy of it." The tie came off and fell to the floor. "Ye resign, do you not?"

"I resign," spluttered the accused, as he turned and ran to the door, wrenched it open and disappeared. The door had not been locked despite the Colonel's command. There was no key.

The Colonel waited until the door slammed shut, dusted his hands and then strode briskly back to his place. "Now," he said. "Any other business?"

As I made my way back to my office I had an uncomfortable feeling that I had seen a similar sequence of events in a film involving Alec Guinness, about a regimental court martial.

The court martial was still in my mind when the next General Committee meeting began to consider the forthcoming Annual Dinner, which was always the event of the Club year. During the meeting, discussion moved to how the guest of honour, a distinguished field marshal, was to be processed formally to the dining room. The Colonel immediately offered to bring his 'personal piper' from Scotland to 'pipe' the field marshal to his place at the top table.

Later that day the Colonel came to my office and explained that it would be necessary to fly his 'personal piper' down from Scotland and he thought the Club should pay the airfare. He said the Chairman was in favour of his proposal. I agreed, as it was the easiest way out.

A few days before the Annual Dinner took place, Matthew popped in to see me. We wandered off to a quiet corner of the

Smoking Room where Matthew ordered two large glasses of Club port. He said, "There are some things you should know about the Colonel."

I waited for him to continue. "The Colonel is not a colonel," he said.

"But he's in the Scots Guards," I countered.

"No," said Matthew, "not the Scots Guards, or any other guards. Not even the fire guards."

"How do you know?" I asked.

Matthew took a deep breath. "I have a day job," he said, "but I have another. It's one that I have to keep quiet. Do you know who I mean by 'six'?"

"I think so," I said.

Matthew took a folder from his inside pocket and spread four or five small colour photos on the table in front of us. They showed various views of a small and impoverished-looking croft. The building was a single storey, low-roofed house, surrounded by several damaged wooden outbuildings. A yard with the odd patch of grass and broken wooden boundary fences provided space for a few wandering chickens.

"Chez Carley," said Matthew. "That's where the Colonel lives and that's the extent of what he calls his land. There are no rolling estates."

Actually, I wasn't entirely surprised.

Matthew continued, taking me through the rest of what he knew of the Colonel. The Colonel, it transpired, had been married several times and each divorce had left him poorer. He really had nothing left and was living on his wits. His membership of the Club was important to him because this gave him a little status and enabled him to maintain some of his former style.

The airfare for his 'personal piper' was, as I had expected, a scam. The money was to pay for the Colonel's journey from Edinburgh. He was finding that his pay as an insurance agent was stretched too thin. The 'personal piper' had been hired from Camden.

It was the final revelation which really shocked me. The Colonel, I had already been told, was not a colonel. The entire sum of his army career amounted to six weeks in the Berkshire Yeomanry, a territorial regiment. After his six weeks' service, Mr Carley had achieved the rank of Acting Second Lieutenant, at which point he had left to take up a two year job selling insurance in New York, allegedly, said Matthew, to avoid National Service.

We agreed that since I wasn't supposed to know what Matthew had told me or how he had obtained his information, it would be better to do nothing but simply watch the 'Colonel's' continuing antics. We did this for some time; and with the knowledge we had, he became quite entertaining.

Unfortunately it all came to a sad end. The new girlfriend's divorce was expensive, and the generous settlement she had expected did not materialise. Despite what she had told her new lover, she had no assets; and neither did he. The lawyer who had acted for them reduced his fee in recognition of a fellow Club member but it was still unachievable. The lawyer reminded his client of the promise to sell his Purdeys.

There were no Purdeys.

****

A selection of the Committee and the Trustees met. They were 'the men in grey suits'. All they knew about the Colonel was that he had defaulted on a fellow member. He had to go.

They called him into one of the committee rooms and told him his fate at nine o'clock on a Friday morning. He took it badly and within the hour he had arrived in my office, weeping, and declaring that the Club was his life. He asked for a triple whisky and I sent for a waiter. He drank his super-large whisky in one go and since the waiter had thoughtfully provided another glass, thinking I might join in the toast, the Colonel took that and downed it. He then set off around the Club intent on saying an increasingly tearful farewell to every Club servant he met.

I thought he was a broken man; but when I encountered him some years later, sitting in the sunshine at the table under the tree in the courtyard behind the Smoking Room, he seemed to have bounced back. I gathered from one of his companions that he might now have become a Brigadier.

The Committee Man

The Committee Man was a splendid fellow. Tall, elegant, articulate and always immaculately dressed in the finest dark blue double-breasted suits that Gieves and Hawkes could produce, his very presence tended to dominate a room. In a world of general scruffiness, his slim frame, clothed in silky fine blue Merino wool with his trademark white silk handkerchief adorning his breast pocket, was hard to miss and even harder to ignore.

The Committee Man knew that the world needed his expertise and his cold, forensic assessment of the ineffective scribblings of his fellows. If it were not for him, minutes would remain inaccurate, stones would remain unturned and society would be enslaved to scoundrels, ever more emboldened by the sure knowledge that their misdemeanours would remain for ever undiscovered.

The Committee Man had certain techniques which had never been known to fail him. He would always sit quietly during the progress of any debate until, at the very end, he would raise a 'point of order' or 'a small matter which had just occurred to him', thus throwing the entirety of the matter under discussion back into the wolverine arena, frustrating the proponents of the motion, exasperating the chairman and causing the remainder of the committee to miss their trains home, their dinners, or their necessary appointments in convenient bars with the best products of Scotland.

The Committee Man was also a consummate actor. When the time came for him to demand the attention of the entire room, he would lean away from the table, remove his gold-framed spectacles and brush his right hand through his thick dark hair which had just the right speckle of grey at the temples as befits a man of maturity and wisdom. He would shake his head and shift the papers on the table in front of him, carefully and successfully choosing his moment to interrupt the current speaker in mid-flow. He would then lift and drop his file of papers with a thump on the polished surface of the table and announce in penetrating theatrical tones, "No, no, no, Chairman, it simply won't do." This would serve both to disrupt the particular point being debated, thus effectively annihilating the preceding arguments, and then to focus the room on what he had decided to say.

The Committee Man never took the chairmanship, vice-chairmanship or any other position of authority. To do so, he believed, would fatally undermine his strategy. How could he tantalise the chairman, disrupt him and finally capture him to use as a puppet for the projection of his own ideas if he were to become the chairman himself?

Of course, the sport would not end with the closure of committee business. The Committee Man would wait gleefully until the minutes were published and then send off a helpful note pointing out a wrongful committee decision, an error in the reported minutes or even a lapse in grammar, demanding that a correction be written and disseminated. In this way, not only could the sport of disruption continue, but the Chairman, wishing to resolve the difficulty as quickly as possible, would soon be brought to do the bidding of the Committee Man – thus frequently changing the impact of the decision previously reached. New minutes would be issued; and, of course, nobody else could challenge them because nobody else had taken sufficiently careful note of the proceedings.

Although he preferred to operate alone, the Committee Man would sometimes feel it necessary to cultivate an ally – never a friend – for a future committee meeting. A glass of sherry in the Drawing Room during a chance encounter would usually suffice – but on occasion this would need to be extended to lunch, thus providing an opportunity to begin the inculcation of the necessary ideas and to set in place a feeling of obligation on the part of the recipient. Elegant but discreet praise, together with a demonstration of intimate knowledge of the circumstances of the target, would overcome the most determined resistance. In this respect, the Committee Man never failed.

The Committee Man was known to everyone but no one actually knew him. That is not to say that they did not know him well, but rather that they did not know him at all. His house was described as a 'Lodge' and evidently did not sink to the ignominy of having a number on the front door. He was known to have been someone important in the city but the amount of time he had been able to spend at leisure suggested that he was no longer in need of gainful employment. It was sometimes suggested, when his name came up in discussion, that he had played rugby for England, or occasionally it might be cricket for England; and he was known to be prominent among the committees of various tennis clubs. He was thought to have links with the nobility; and this was emphasised by his habit of referring to princes and earls on first name terms or – more often – by using a nickname known only to the few of an inner circle. On very rare occasions he had been heard to request a companion not to use his own title, but no one knew what that title might be.

He was undoubtedly well-connected, and was able to infer acquaintance with any public personage whose name might crop up, even, or perhaps especially, royalty. Military distinction was also believed to have come his way, and when the opportunity seemed appropriate he was introduced with the rank of 'Major', probably, it was thought, in the Household Division.

The Committee Man was well-versed in the protocol to be observed at Royal Garden Parties and seemed familiar with the interiors of both Windsor Castle and the Palace of Holyroodhouse in Edinburgh, as well as making occasional nostalgic reference to the former Royal Yacht *Britannia.*

His casual companions, of which there were few, and his acquaintances, of which there were many, were impressed by the number and range of his appointments but noted that his interest always seemed to lie with influential committees; and some wondered at the absence of any reference to a seat on a Board.   This was soon explained in that seats on Boards generally implied remuneration and it had been recognised early on that such benefit would have been utterly beneath the status of the Committee Man, who never mentioned money and who seemed to regard the subject as rather grubby.

In fact, although being very well-known and with a wide circle of respectful acquaintances, the Committee Man had no friends – and this was a circumstance he regarded as essential to his way of life and his continued well-being.

The Committee Man had spent many hours building a persona which was actually a myth. He had learned, over a period of several years, the value of shaping images which were so impressive and so mysterious that others were drawn to the ephemera in the hope of learning more before being trained into subservience and awe. At this point, particularly within the comfort of a group, most men were sufficiently malleable to be useful to a further expansion of the image. The Committee Man had learnt these and other secrets of human frailty and psychology at the feet of masters. The first of these masters had begun to groom the future Committee Man in the confines of Wormwood Scrubs until the pupil had graduated to the softer and fresher environment of Ford Open Correction Centre. Later, spells in Strangeways and finally Peterhead had honed the skills of manipulation to such a degree that the

Committee Man was ready in all respects to go forth and assist the world.

The Committee Man had learned the value of the deed poll process in the establishment of new identities and had acquired the skill of hand necessary to provide the small necessities of life without always resorting to the irritation of payment.

The 'Lodge' had never been a traditional fixed building. In his early days, the Committee Man had enjoyed the convenience and mobility of a motor caravan; but in more recent times this had morphed into a rather stylish narrowboat, presently moored to the embankment of one of the more fashionable parts of the Regents Canal. The 'Lodge' had occupied its present berth for nearly six months and detailed plans were already in place for a move by progressive steps to a comfortable marina berth on the Thames near Teddington. The Committee Man had also found it useful to obtain possession of a small farmhouse surrounded by an uncultivated smallholding near the river Cher in the Loire region of France. It was here that some of his more sensitive exchanges took place and it also presented him with the ability to disappear from his usual haunts in and around London, emerging in the farmhouse with a completely different persona and a passport showing him to be a Belgian national. In France he spoke no English and in London he spoke no French.

If pressed beyond his usual reticence to discuss what he did for a living, the Committee Man would describe himself as a communications consultant. But of course such admissions were rare and likely to be shrouded in confusion and inference rather than fact. The Committee Man was always protected by his skill of entering a group conversation with an assertion just sufficiently contentious to embolden the conversation so that he needed only to listen, occasionally raising an eyebrow, frowning, or saying "Quite so."

It was true that in this manner the Committee Man did make his living from communication. He listened. This technique enabled him to become the temporary custodian of information which should have enjoyed the protection of discretion and which could have significant value, given the right circumstances and the right customers. Like a prospector panning for gold, the Committee Man would sift and sort the information which, often inadvertently, came his way. When he had a package which might have a value, he would consider and carefully select the person or organisation which would be likely to extract the best value from the package and therefore offer him a reasonable return for his research.

The Committee Man usually worked through intermediaries in the recovery of valuable but small items such as jewellery. However he had been known, in his earlier and younger days, to experience the thrill of lifting from a dressing table a bracelet or necklace which would be unlikely to be missed immediately by the owner simply because it was surrounded by so many other valuables. Frequently, when the loss was discovered and more time wasted in frantic searches, the owner would delay even longer before facing the anger of a spouse.

By the age of sixty the Committee Man had amassed so much wealth that he could easily retire from the lucrative business he had built up. He made plans to fade away from the scenes where he was known so well; but habit and the expectation of the little thrill that accompanied each success drew him back time and again. He retained tremendous self-belief and as he grew older this encouraged him to take a few more risks. They were never big risks and he could easily explain any odd behaviour, using as his final weapon the application of lofty contempt and disdain.

His mistake, when it came, was in paying insufficient attention to what he described as 'Staff' or more frequently – and usually in private but always with a sneer – as 'the hired hands' or 'the hirelings'. However, privacy is generally a protection shot full of holes, requiring an interloper merely to find those holes.

The drab secretary who took the minutes at several of the meetings was a person with the ability to blend into his surroundings, becoming almost a part of the furniture so that when the meeting was being wrapped up and shortly afterwards, people forgot he was there. He was a quiet bachelor with time on his hands and, at home, he used this time to solve puzzles. He was an avid puzzler and had developed a forensic skill which under different circumstances might have made him a great detective. As well as recording committee proceedings, his duties included a number of other functions; and in support of these his duties took him all over the establishment. All of the Committee members were so used to his presence that frequently they were unaware that he was in the same room. It was in this way that he overheard a group of three men comparing their experiences of thefts which they and friends had suffered over a period of five years or so. The talk was not much more than a comparison of responses by insurance companies, each story seemingly being slightly embellished to out-do the previous one. The secretary found himself casually wondering why so many men, evidently from the same social circles, seemed to have been the victims of theft and why the thefts all seemed to involve small, well-insured and highly valuable items. There were, of course, many other victims of similar thefts but the secretary was unaware of this, and the interesting problem became a puzzle.

The secretary made it his business to listen more carefully as he attended to his duties and he heard other groups discussing the loss of small but very valuable items. When he returned late in the evening to his cramped, dingy flat in Battersea he would frequently open a bottle of beer and sit and worry at his new puzzle well into the small hours; and it was not long before a pattern began to emerge. Thefts took place in the extended period of months following a series of meetings. During the summer and at other times when there were fewer or no meetings, thefts continued but differed in style and location. In part, of course, this might have been because information supplied some time beforehand was only now being acted upon.

The secretary was an honest man and he decided to take his suspicions discreetly to the Chairman of one of the principal committees. The Chairman, an elderly avuncular man, added his own suspicions and read more into what he was being told than the teller intended.

The Chairman was well-connected in a number of disparate spheres.

It was three weeks after the last meeting of the Committee of Ways and Means when the body was found. It must have been hit by one of the last trains running through Charing Cross Underground. There were no witnesses to the accident and it was presumed that the victim must have been standing too close to the platform edge and had somehow missed his footing.

The body was unrecognisable as a human being and it was eventually identified by a file containing the committee minutes which was found in a damaged but still recognisable briefcase which lay beside the live rail. The Committee Man had many acquaintances but seemed to have no friends or family. It was an acquaintance who later formally identified the body lying in the refrigerated drawer; but the formal identification was really based on the papers in the briefcase, rather than the pathetic shrunken figure in the refrigerated cabinet.

The funeral was a very grand affair, but curiously, no immediate family could be located and no one seemed to have been sufficiently close to the deceased to be able to put together a eulogy appropriate to a man of so many talents and such distinction. It was left to the Honorary Chaplain who was able to ramble on for ten minutes about dry sherry, fine wines, handwriting, eloquence and an air of culture.   Only the Honorary Chaplain attended the Committal.

The End